PEWTER

John Bedford

WALKER AND COMPANY
NEW YORK

Library of Congress Catalog Card Number: 66–22380

First published in the United States of America in
1966 by Walker and Company, a division of
Publications Development Corporation
Third Printing 1968

Printed in Great Britain

Contents

Introduction

This little book is addressed not to the specialized pewter collector but to those who are curious to know why there should be pewter collectors at all. It is not a spectacular metal like silver or gold, it does not hold the high brilliance of coloured enamels, and it has nothing of the soft delicacy of porcelain. Wherein, therefore, lies its attraction?

Gilbert wrote:

> The end is easily foretold:
> When every blessed thing you hold
> Is made of silver, or of gold,
> You long for simple pewter.

Pewter, especially English pewter, is indeed simple, and its soft subdued texture and colour has no exact counterpart in any other material. Today furniture collectors are looking again at the carved oak of the Renaissance or the simple pieces of the country farmhouse or cottage. They will find that pewter consorts with these things as admirably as it ever did.

In the same way it finds a sympathetic home in rooms which again show plain wood: the brilliant scarlets and blues we now prefer to recent drabness might have been specially selected to show off the unique light of pewter.

For those who find the old English forms too simple and austere, there is always the highly decorated work of the Continent, or the astonishing variety of things made around the turn of this century in the spirit of Art Nouveau. And for the Autolycuses of this world, the snappers-up of unconsidered trifles, there are enough curiosities and bygones to keep them busy collecting for a lifetime.

1. Pewter and Pewterers

If you are going to start collecting pewter it will be reasonable to ask what it is. You will find that there are several answers, all of which can be right.

Somewhere in remote antiquity it will have been observed that with a small amount of tin added to copper you had an alloy which was much harder than copper itself, and which could easily be cast and worked to a smooth surface. This was bronze, and its discovery gave birth to a whole age and culture. Then—perhaps by another happy accident —someone reversed the proportions of tin and copper; and just as bronze was more practicable than straight copper, so this new lighter alloy was more useful than straight tin, which did not flow easily and yet was too soft for convenient working. As time went on other ingredients than copper were added to the tin—lead, antimony, bismuth, etc., all of which gave the alloy various desirable qualities: so that after some centuries of evolution there came into being in medieval and Renaissance Europe what can perhaps without too much exaggeration be called the Pewter Age.

CLASSICAL PEWTER

Only in English, apparently, is the word 'pewter' used for the various alloys: we seem to have taken it from the Italian *peltro*. Elsewhere the word 'tin' appears in its various forms —in France *étain*, in Germany and the Netherlands *zinn*. Thus, when Homer described the 'tin' shield of Achilles he may well have been talking of a pewter alloy, as may Aristotle in his reference to the statue of Dædalus. Plutus mentions dishes of the same material which could not possibly have been pure tin and the same applies to the recommendation by Galen, father of medicine, for its use, along with silver and glass, as a suitable material in which to keep antidotes and drugs.

That pewter was made all through classical times is evidenced in the museum collections, and perhaps the craft never really disappeared even in the Dark Ages. But it was in the early Renaissance that it really came to full flowering. Where the peasants used wooden platters and the great nobles gold and silver plate, the mass of the middle and upper classes, the trade guilds and the churches, expressed their increasing sophistication and wealth by using fine pewter for display and a lesser sort for everyday use.

Evidently England played a leading part in this process. When the tin-mines of Spain became submerged in the Moorish conquest of the eighth century, our own Cornwall—the Phoenicians' 'Cassiterides' or 'Land of Tin'—became the principal source of supply of pewter's most important constituent.

It is more than likely that the still-existing Roman pieces were made of tin from the ancient Duchy; and this dominance may well have continued right down to the days when tin was discovered in huge and more easily accessible quantities in Malaya; and also after pewter, for general use, had been superseded by pottery and glass.

PEWTERERS' GUILDS

Although some kind of trade organization must have existed throughout the Middle Ages, the Pewterers' Company first achieved official recognition in the year 1348, during the reign of Edward III. Ordinances were drawn up by the members of the trade and submitted for the approval of the Lord Mayor and Aldermen.

Collectors will find it enormously helpful, and in fact imperative, to study these Ordinances. They determined the types of wares made, specified the alloys authorized for the different kinds of article, laid down rules for making them, and set up standards to which all members of the Guild had to conform. These were obviously aimed at protecting

6

respectable and honest members of the trade from the unfair competition of their less reputable brethren and also from outsiders apt to undercut them with inferior work.

In the first place [runs a modern transliteration of the Ordinances] seeing that the trade of pewtery is founded upon certain matters and metals, such as copper, tin and lead, in due proportions: of which three metals they make vessels, that is to say pots, salers [salt-cellars] esquelles [bowls], platters and other things by good folk bespoken: the which things cannot be made without good knowledge of the pewterer expert and cunning in the craft: (seeing that so many persons not knowing the right alloys, nor yet the mixtures or the right rules of the trade, do work and make vessels and other things not in due manner, to the damage of the people and to the scandal of the trade) therefore the good folk of the trade do pray that it may be ordained that three or four of the most true and cunning in the craft be chosen to oversee the alloys and workmanship aforesaid: and that by their examination and assay amendment may speedily be made where default has been committed.

German guild cup, dated 1768.
(Victoria & Albert Museum)

7

The Ordinances go on to regulate the alloys proper to different articles, to lay down rules for taking on apprentices and workmen, defining the places and times where pewter may be made—working at night was strictly forbidden—and many other points. Penalties were severe, amounting ultimately to virtual outlawry:

> Also, as to those of the trade who shall be found working otherwise than is before set forth, and upon assay shall be found guilty; upon the first default let them lose the material so wrought: upon the second default let them lose the material and suffer punishment at the discretion of the Mayor and Aldermen; and if a third time they shall be found offending let them forswear the craft for evermore.

Nevertheless the Worshipful Company of Pewterers, like the other trade guilds of the age, were by no means a soulless trade association laying down laws.

In the progression from apprentice to journeyman and master working on his own account, there was a kind of paternalism, with religious and social bonds all the way up the ladder.

A boy would be apprenticed for seven years or more, during which time he would live in his master's household and accompany him to church on Sundays and holidays. Having served his time he would be presented by his master for swearing in as a Freeman, submitted to an examination and sometimes obliged to show a 'proof piece' as testimony of his skill.

The new Freeman could then either continue working for his former master or go off as a journeyman: and after some years, when he had acquired enough skill and capital, he could set up on his own account, registering his 'touch' (see pages 13–14). Only then could he apply to be elected a Liveryman, and so qualify himself as a member of the

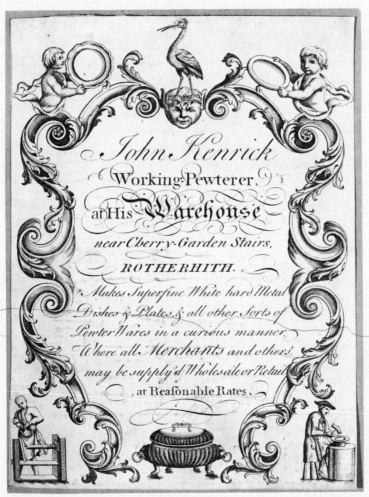

Trade Card of John Kenrick of London, who was elected to the Freedom or Yeomanry in 1737, and became Renter Warden in 1754. His touch mark, showing a stork, is No. 885 on the London Touchplate. (British Musenm)

9

Court and become eligible for office in the Company, perhaps progressing the whole way from the Livery to Stewardship, the Court of Assistants, Renter Warden, Upper Warden and finally Mastership.

In this world, strikes or lock-outs were totally irrelevant. The guilds and companies in Britain and on the Continent existed as tightly organized units whose only care was to get the best possible deal for all its members against all outsiders—including the buying public.

IN THE PROVINCES

Outside London, the pewterers either set up guilds of their own, or in the smaller places associated themselves with allied trades. The records of Ordinances of the Pewterers' Guild of York date from 1419, and those of Bristol from 1456. At King's Lynn the pewterers appear among the Freemen from 1445 to 1446 and at Norwich they were members of the St Luke's Guild from 1449. At Edinburgh (1496), Ludlow (1511), Perth (1546), Aberdeen (1519), Dundee (1587), Stirling (1605), and Glasgow (1648) they were found among the 'Hammermen'; and at Dublin (1556), Hull (1598), Cork (1656), and Youghal (1657) they were in the Guild of Smiths. In 1536 they were to be found as members of the Company of Goldsmiths, Plumbers, Glaziers, Pewterers and Painters of Newcastle upon Tyne. Other centres where there seems to be evidence of pewter-making include Bewdley (Worcestershire), Exeter, Sunderland, Yarmouth, Barnstable, Birmingham, Chester, Liverpool, Manchester, and Wigan.

As in England, the continental pewterers early petitioned their authorities to regulate the trade and eliminate the competition of cheap shoddy wares with excessive amounts of lead, which was dangerous to the health of both workers and the public. Guilds came into existence early in the fifteenth century, sometimes allied to other trades such as the Smiths', sometimes, as in England, on their own.

Some typical marks (see page 14).

FINE AND COMMON PEWTER

The early Ordinances, as has been noted, laid down the standards of alloy for the various products. Porringers, saucers, platters, chargers, 'and other things that are made square or cistils [ribbed]' had to be made of what was called 'fine' pewter. This meant such a proportion of copper to tin 'as of its own nature it will take': it worked out at about 26 lbs. of copper to 112 lbs. of tin or, in some cases, tin and brass in the proportions of $4\frac{1}{13}$ to 1. All other vessels, such as rounded pots, cruets, candlesticks, etc., could be wrought of tin alloyed with lead 'in reasonable proportions' —which were considered to be 22 lbs. of lead to 112 lbs. of tin.

The highest-priced alloy now known in the trade is 'tin and temper', an alloy of tin with copper and antimony, but pewterers in modern times have tended to be rather reticent about the exact proportions of their alloys. In the early 1900s Liberty's were using for their decorative wares (see page 62) a pewter where tin was alloyed in the proportion of 'five per cent of antimony or bismuth or both'. Other authorities speak of Trifle, or 'common' pewter, as being composed of 82/83 parts tin to 17/18 of antimony; there is also what is known as 'Pemberton's alloy', which is 90 parts tin to 10 of antimony.

'Ordinary' pewter is characterized by a still existing pewterer as an alloy of tin, antimony and lead, 'and the more lead the lower the quality'. Some qualities are by these standards very low indeed. Ley or 'lay metal' was 80 parts tin to 20 of lead or more. Roman pewter has been analysed and shown to be roughly 3 parts tin to 1 part lead, while if one takes a dive into the pot-houses of Victorian times one finds 'black-metal', which sank as low as 60 parts tin to 40 of lead. This was a dangerously high proportion of lead, a fact which was recognized by legislation first in France, then (in 1907) in England. In both countries the upper limit of lead was put at 10%, while here the proportion of 80% of tin was insisted upon also.

There is an alloy called *Silberzinn*, which has sometimes been credited with having silver in it: but Mr Cotterell points out that no such thing was permitted by the Ordinances of any known guild. The light silvery colour may be due to the use of lead of a slightly argentiferous nature.

MAKING AND DECORATION

Pewter articles are made by melting the alloy and casting it in moulds, by hammering the metal when it has been produced in plate form, and by turning on a lathe and burnishing. There may also be combinations of these methods, according to the type of piece or the result required. The serious pewter collector will learn to recognize the marks of these various techniques and this will help to distinguish the genuine from the fake, the unsullied original from the 'improved'.

English pewter is, on the whole, much plainer and simpler than continental, relying mainly upon beauty of outline and high quality of manufacture. Why this should be so is something of a mystery, for it was true of pewter made long before the austerities of the Puritan Age.

Nevertheless there is decoration of a restrained kind,

chiefly in what is called 'wriggled work'. Here the engraver uses a chisel-like tool of various widths, and, holding it at an angle to the surface of the piece, makes a cut by rocking the tool from side to side. This technique is more suited to pewter than engraving, as used on silver, for the metal is much softer and a deep cut is not wanted: the work also stands up better to the inevitable wear in cleaning. There is engraving with a burin, usually where a coat of arms has been drawn on the edge of a plate; and some rare pieces are punched with dies, especially where lettering has been done, and patterns are created by using different shaped dies. There is also some etching which is quite pleasing in its effect. Pewter takes kindly to embossing, and some fine simple patterns have been worked out.

Intricate cast decoration is rarely found in England: for example, on the unique Grainger Candlestick shown on page 51. For this work one has to turn to the continental *Edelzinn*, or 'noble pewter' of the sixteenth and seventeenth centuries. These highly intricate castings, sometimes so shallow as to be taken for engraving, are really goldsmiths' work—as indeed is hinted in the French expression *orfèvrerie d'étain*. The work of the pieces made from moulds engraved by the Frenchman François Briot and the Germans Caspar Enderlein and Jacob Koch, among others, may be seen in the continental museums.

There is pewter which has been given a coating of coloured lacquer, and engraved with a pattern showing the metal through. The coffee urn on page 61 has another type of painting, as used in *tôle peinte*, familiar to us as Pontypool ware. A great deal of this work was done in France and the Netherlands at the end of the eighteenth century and the beginning of the nineteenth, usually on pewter of inferior quality.

MARKS

It has already been noted that when a pewterer set up on his own he was required to register his 'touch'—that is to say, a mark impressed with a die or punch which was kept on a collective plate at Pewterers' Hall, and also displayed upon his own premises. This mark had always to be struck upon his wares, so that they could be identified.

Many and varied are the marks so used, and collectors of early wares were dealt a cruel blow by the disappearance in the Great Fire of London of the plates bearing the touches of pewterers up until that time. However, after the Fire, touches of the surviving pewterers were struck again, and the custom has been kept up ever since.

The Pewterers' Company now possess five touchplates, bearing 1,000 touches. They are all shown in such standard works as H. H. Cotterell's *Old Pewter, Its Makers and Marks*, which also contains a register showing the names and other particulars of most of the pewterers to whom they refer. Surviving Edinburgh touchplates run from 1580 to 1764.

Besides the devices used by the pewterers for their touches, other marks appear on pewter. There is the Rose and Crown, which seems to have been an official attestation of good quality—like the hall-mark in silver. The Crowned X signified a special hard quality of pewter: and as used on the Continent it referred to an alloy of 10 parts pewter to 1 part lead—perhaps this was the significance of the 'X'. Then there was a whole range of symbols and words much more like our modern trade-marks: some of these are shown here. Also to be found on some early pieces are marks similar to those on hall-marked silver, sometimes deceptively so—like those of the modern electro-platers. Capacity marks upon measures are mentioned on page 35.

CLEANING AND REPAIRING

Pewter collectors seem to be divided into two races, those who like their possessions to have the full brilliance of the new article, and those who prefer to let them fall into the dull grey tones of age, even bearing the scars of wear and oxidization.

The wisest course, perhaps, is to steer somewhere between

Edinburgh Touchplate showing approximate dates of marks. (National Museum of Antiquities of Scotland, Edinburgh)

these alternatives. Now that we no longer use our show pewter for eating and drinking there is no point in scouring it, as did our forebears: and the removal of a fine old patina would be a crime indeed. We will obviously want to remove or have removed the hideous marks of corrosion: and there seems to be no reason in the world why one should not have breaks repaired and dents tapped out.

Mr Cotterell recommends that for heavily corroded pieces 1 lb. of caustic soda should be dissolved in 4 gallons of boiling water, then the pewter boiled in it for two or three hours, taking care to put something like a piece of cloth between the pewter and the bottom of the vessel, so that it will not get too hot: afterwards it should be cleaned with the finest 'Calais sand or Monkey soap', and given a final polish with powdered rotten stone, whitening, or any other plate powder or polish. Alternatively he suggests washing in soap and water and painting all over the surface with a 50% solution of hypochloric acid (spirits of salts), leaving this on for a few minutes and cleaning off with the finest emery-powder and water. That most entertaining writer and collector Mr Charles Rowed, after getting into serious trouble with his family for ruining all their saucepans, took to using an old bath into which he put a boiled solution of 2 oz. rock lime, 2 oz. caustic soda, 6 oz. common salt, 8 oz. common soda and 3 quarts of water, adding 8 quarts of cold water. He steeped as many pieces of pewter in this as the water would cover, and found that the corrosion could then easily be wiped off.

But many collectors prefer to entrust their pieces to the specialist dealers, who know their business thoroughly.

2. Tankards, Flagons, and Measures

In its early days the tankard seems to have been thought of as a measure, and some still rather mysterious names are to be found attached to them in the Ordinances of the Pewterers. In the days of James I (James VI of Scotland) we find references to such things as 'thurndells' (or thurrendales, thurdendales) either 'new fashion' or 'hooped', which are evidently measures of capacity. This measure, it is thought, was three pints, but we have no Elizabethan or early Jacobean pots to prove it. There are also 'Winchester' quarts and pints; there are 'Ephram' or 'Ephraim' pots in sizes from three quarts to a half-pint; and 'Danske' pots, with or without lids.

These seem to have marked the beginning, perhaps, of the flat-topped late Stuart tankard, for those of the Commonwealth period tended to be squatter.

STYLES OF COMPONENTS

In tracing the development of the tankard, and placing specimens in their periods, much guidance is to be found in the shapes and styles of the various parts—the body or drum, the lid, thumbpiece and the handle. It must be borne in mind, however, that these different styles overlapped each other: the appearance of a new one did not necessarily mean the extinction of another. Moulds were expensive items in the trade, and were not discarded lightly.

BODY SHAPES

Tankards with dome tops first appeared in the 1680s, the earliest having a tooth-edged serration in the upper lid, but the characteristic vessel of the time was the extremely graceful flat-lidded tankard. The earliest forms, with some exceptions, show a squat body and pronounced entasis, or

Tankards. **(Left)** *Last quarter seventeenth century. Engraved with a cypher and the portraits of William III and Mary II. Maker's touch 'R.S.' crowned.* (Right) *Late eighteenth century. Engraved with initials 'IAM' beneath an anchor. Touch of Pitt and Dudley, London. 8⅝ ins. high.* (Victoria & Albert Museum)

taper, from bottom to top. The drum may be plain, and later (say in the reign of William and Mary) acquire a skirted base and a fillet a little way up.

This form continued to be made uninterruptedly, although later in taller forms. Then about 1725 there appeared the two shapes which were to compete strenuously with the cylindrical and sometimes oust it entirely from popular favour. These were the 'bell' and the 'tulip', which carried on throughout the nineteenth century with a more pronounced 'belly'. The earliest tulip-shape was particularly popular with the West Country pewterers: Mr Cotterell says that eight of every ten he examined were found to bear the mark of either a Bristol or Exeter maker.

LIDS OR COVERS

Cover or lid styles are of the highest significance in dating tankards. The earliest of all—again with the usual excep-

Tankard drums. Skirted base (seventeenth century), bell and tulip (mid eighteenth century and 1800 onwards) (see also pp. 26 and 27).

tions—is the flat top of the early Stuart period, 'pinched' to a point in front for pouring, as with pottery. The sides of the raised centre are vertical, but about 1650 there set in a fashion whereby convex mouldings were placed under the top to support the raised centre, to give a flattened 'bun' shape—and in fact this word is used to describe the

style. Together with this innovation came another: the 'pinched' front was superseded by a serrated brim projection or forelip. Yet another style which got under way in this same reign, and which was to dominate lidded tankards for the rest of time in England, was the 'double-domed'. Here the raised mouldings start at the outside edge with a pronounced curve: this type has been dated from about 1715.

HANDLES

Handles play an important part not only in the aesthetic appearance of tankards, but in suggesting the approximate date. The very earliest pots showed a primitive version in which the top end of the handle tended to cant up at the point where it became attached to the body. Other early Stuart pots had a slender handle, with a fishtail end coming very low on the body, sometimes only just clearing the table. But about 1655 the top end acquired a long 'V' piece which

Tankard lids. Early seventeenth century; late seventeenth century; early double-domed and later double-domed (early eighteenth century onwards).

ran down the back of the drum; and this 'beak' together with the graceful sweep of the handle, earned for the shape the name 'swan's neck'. Nothing could be more satisfying than the relationship between this handle, the squatly tapering drum and the broad-rimmed flat lid overlapping all: for me it makes the Stuart tankard the most beautiful of all made in England, perhaps anywhere.

Running about fifteen years later in both cases, and appearing with the earliest double-domed covers, came a modification of the 'swan's neck' without the 'V'. This also had variations in the terminal, perhaps with a 'heel' or small shield at the end, an ogee curve, a spiral or a ball.

From now on these handles started to pick up the more flowing curves of the Baroque and the Rococo, first developing an 'S' curve and becoming much heavier, then turning themselves into a double handle. Here one or both ends were fastened to the drum by a strut—which for many collectors has been a most unpewterly feature, for they feel it is more properly silversmiths' work. But the style lasted for a century and a half, well into the nineteenth century, and perhaps was symptomatic of the decline of pewter into an imitation of the more costly metal.

But along with the double handle one also finds pieces with a swan's neck shape but having a dished piece for the thumb where the top enters the drum, and sometimes a fishtail and 'tuft'.

Tankard handles. Second half seventeenth century; early to mid eighteenth century; mid eighteenth to mid nineteenth century; two examples late eighteenth to mid nineteenth century; 1800 onwards; and Scotland, say, 1780 to 1825.

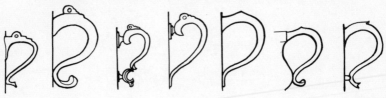

Group of pewter tankards and measures from the Chequers, Lamberhurst, Kent.

THUMBPIECES

Finally there is the thumbpiece, sometimes called a billet, purchase or lever. The shape and setting of this can again be vital to the appearance of the tankard. Earliest of them, but more often found on flagons than tankards, is the 'twin-dome' or 'twin-cup', a very beautiful type made of two small cups side by side. But the prevailing type used all through the Stuart period and for some years into the eighteenth century was what has generically been called the 'double volute', but which seems to divide itself again into sub-types. One family appears as a 'ram's horn'; another looks like a 'fleur-de-lis'; but there are many variations of both. In this era one also finds a type which shows two love-birds under the volutes: while versions found on the larger measures suggest the three feathers of the Prince of Wales's crest.

In Georgian days there appeared the later types such as the 'chairback' and the 'open', this latter eventually superseding all the others. Once again, time was not very kind to pewter.

Lidless tankards are to be found from the earliest days, and very pleasing they are. They seem to have a more pronounced entasis than the lidded ones, and are also much slimmer: these factors make them sit upon a table with admirable character, especially when they have hooped bands or other decoration.

'PUB' TANKARDS
From as far back as the late seventeenth century there are tankards engraved with names and often dates—or marks which enable one to place them within a few years. They often immortalize some long-vanished inn and its keeper, such as 'Edward Hill at ye Red Lion in ye Poultry, 1670' or 'John Wallhope att the Bell att Turvey, 1703'. Sometimes they bear the initials of the landlord and his wife arranged in a triangle; or some such warning as 'If sold stole'.

Excise marks appear on them, although sometimes in a confusing sequence, which suggests that they may have been 'stole', and travelled about the country, so picking up the marks of different districts.

They are the progenitors of the Victorian 'pub' tankard, still to be found in odd corners, or unearthed during building operations. Here the inn name is usually to be found on the bottoms, the latter apparently formed not with punches but by simple cuts which have afterwards been joined with small touches. These pots were once despised by serious collectors because of the low standard of their metal, but like so many other things of late date they now have their enthusiasts, and many a one has found its way back to its original home.

EARLY TALL FLAGONS
If the English tankard began life small and squat, the flagon first appeared in a tall, graceful form. But it is often very difficult to distinguish between them.

One hears of Elizabethan round-bellied or baluster flagons like those in silver, but the type did not apparently stand up to the hazard of getting crushed down into the foot. More typical of the early seventeenth century was the tapering body, perhaps 13–14 ins. high, with a splayed foot

Two tankards. (Left) *With clear and tinted glass base.* (Right) *Engraved 'Chequers Hotel, Lamberhurst'.*

rim, a flattened bun-shaped cover or more rarely a double-dome, often with a finial, a swan-necked handle, and quite often the twin-cusped thumbpiece. There is also another cover shaped more like a 'muffin' and thus named, as well as the attractive 'beefeater', so called because of its resemblance to the cap of the Yeoman of the Guard. The 'beefeater' flagon also usually has the spreading base which came in at the mid-century.

Some flagons might be 15–16 ins. tall, while Wiltshire's 'Pot of Fishertonanger', dated 1660, soars to 21½ ins. Towards the end of the Stuart period, the flat-topped lid of the tankard appears also on flagons, and similarly is succeeded by the double-domed. One sometimes sees the high dome familiar in Queen Anne silver teapots, a likeness which is taken even further in the Scottish 'pot-bellied' flagon, like the pair in Brechin Cathedral.

One of the most interesting—as well as the rarest—is the York flagon, unique to that city and very rare: Mr Cotterell thought there might be twenty in existence—four of which are in York Museum. It is shaped like an acorn—often having a smaller acorn as a finial—has a deep lip and a massive thumbpiece. A fine shape, one regrets that it was not produced at more centres. Incidentally it was not the only shape produced at York; there are straight-sided types with flat Stuart lids and early Georgian types with double-domed lids and fishtail handles.

Gourde or pilgrim bottle. German, dated 1661, 13⅞ ins. high. (Victoria & Albert Museum)

From the mid eighteenth century come the 'broken' handles and the 'chairback' thumbpieces to be found on contemporary tankards, also the double-curved handles with struts of the period of decadence.

A type particularly associated with Ireland shows the wide base of the 'beefeater' together with a domed cover and a large full-curved handle not seen elsewhere. Scotland's original contribution has a tapering drum, slightly incurved, also a dished cover. The Scots liked to put a band of reeding round the middle of the drum, also to give it a very plain and dignified handle.

British flagons were used for both secular and sacred purposes. The latter often bear an inscription naming the donor and the church to which it was given. But uninscribed ones may well have found their way out of a church into the market-place.

CONTINENTAL FLAGONS

When we turn to continental flagons and tankards we find once again that the distinction between the two tends to get blurred. The names are even more confusing. If the word tankard derived originally from the Latin *cantharus—*

a large goblet with handles—we get the French *canette*, and the Germanic forms *Kanne*, *Kane*, *Kan*, etc., but these are used of pieces which we would call flagons. There are also such terms as *Krug*, *Pitsche*, *aiguière*, which suggest ewer or jug forms, while *gourde* seems to strike out into entirely fresh ground.

Here is a short account of some of them:

Aiguière-en-Casque. The helmet-shaped ewer, often seen in silver and gold.

Bernese Wine Can. This handsome vessel is a ewer with a bulbous body, a narrow waist and a long straight spout with 'frilled' decoration.

Biberon. Not much like the glass vessel of the same name, but the Swiss *Brunkessis* (see page 26), which looks like, but is not, a kettle. In fact it functions rather like a baby's bottle in that one sucks rather than drinks from it. The tube-like spout goes down nearly to the bottom of the vessel, so that the liquid may be drained without disturbing the sediment on the top.

Cemaire, Cemaise. This very grand ceremonial flagon, used as a presentation piece for distinguished guests or conquerors, is usually on a swinging handle or chain.

Cologne Flagon. A baluster-shaped vessel with a central dome arising from the flat lid.

Gourde. Almost every material, from the clay of ancient Sumer to the glass of nineteenth-century Nailsea, has its version of this vessel, sometimes known as a pilgrim's flask. It normally has a flat, round, disc-like shape and a pair of earpieces, which together make it the handiest vessel

German Pechkrug, or pitch tankard, of wood and pewter. Late eighteenth century. (Victoria & Albert Museum)

Tankards or Flagons. Swiss Brunkessis or Biberon, Scottish Pot-bellied, Jan Steen, York, Rembrandt, and English Communion.

known to man for the personal carrying of water, whether he rides an Arabian charger, walks on rag-bound feet from city to city in search of alms or marches across deserts with great armies. Sometimes gourdes get themselves up on high feet, but more often they have a stand of a peculiar shape which has been likened to a ploughshare. Gourdes are very much of the Gothic era, often bearing the arms of German knights of the fourteenth century and earlier. Sometimes the gourde discards its ears or lugs and acquires a handle and a hinged lid, perhaps with a heart-shaped device under the lip. There are also gourdes which are as bulbous as the fruit, whose scooped-out sun-dried case, drawn together at the neck with string, was the grandfather of them all. When one swings from chains, as does that on page 24, it presumably qualifies as a *Cemaire* (q.v.).

Gut. Not a pleasant name but it comes from the Latin *guttus*, and is a narrow-necked vessel with a screw top and ring. This was to enable it to be lowered into a well or a stream, so keeping its contents cool: most German wines drink the better for this. Those with spouts are for must, the syrup left in the vat after the clear wine has been drawn off: their spouts usually have lids as well.

Guild Tankards or Flagons (see page 7). These are the great

vessels standing 20 ins. high or more which were used at meetings of the trade guilds, not only of the pewterers themselves, but also of all the other crafts. They usually bear some appropriate emblematic figure such as a lamb for the clothworkers, a horse for blacksmiths, a mallet and square for masons, bones and cleavers for butchers, fish for fishmongers and shoes for shoemakers. They may also have lion masks as decoration, also one or more shields or medallions bearing the names of officers of the guild. But many of these additions were made in later days.

Hanap. Another name for the *Guild Tankard* (q.v.).

Hanseatic Flagon. A baluster shape in two main types, one low and thick-set, the other tall and slender. It is held that the heavy-bottomed type, like the Rodney glass decanters of Georgian England, were used on shipboard, in vessels sailing out of the Hanseatic ports, and were made thus so that they would stand firm against the rolling of the ship: many of them have, in fact, been found in waterways.

's Hertogenbosch Tankard. A short and squat type which bears the arms either of this Netherlands town or of some other place.

Humpen. Glass collectors will find this a familiar term: in pewter it describes the magnificent flagons associated with guilds, otherwise *Guild Tankards* (q.v.).

Jan Steen. From the frequency with which this Netherlands painter showed them in his work, flagons of a certain type (see page 26) with a domed lid and a long square spout have come to be called after him. But many other artists of

the time have depicted the same shape: and this is perhaps
as good a place as anywhere to recommend tyro collectors
to look carefully among the details of works by Old Masters,
which taken together make a fine illustrated catalogue of the
best pewter.

Höhlpfennige. Cup-shaped coins (literally 'hollow pennies')
which were used to close the top of the peg in the lids of
certain types of Hanseatic and North German flagons; and
thus useful in determining the place of origin of such pieces.

Kindbettschüsseli. What in England would be called a caudle
cup (see page 41). It is literally a 'childbed cup' in which
gruel was carried to expectant or nursing mothers. Very
much of the eighteenth century and not much seen today.

Lamb's Flagon. A baluster flagon with a strut connecting the
body to the long spout. Said to have been used for (a) lambs,
and (b) invalids.

Pechkrug (see page 25). Literally a 'pitch-jug', that is to say,
built of wooden pitch-lined staves in the manner of barrels;
but they are banded with decorative pieces of pewter
instead of willow wands and they have pewter lids and
fittings. They represent strikingly the transition from 'treen'
or wooden drinking vessels to those in pewter; and seem to
come only from Thuringia and the Scandinavian countries.

Pitsche. One of the most frequently seen items in continental
pewter today, these are the simple wine-cans used by the
German peasant for centuries. They come in all manner of
shapes, sometimes even in the form of a book; and there is
a ring in the lid for lowering into water (cf. *Gut*).

Ratskanne. A council or town-hall flagon, and therefore
something of a grandee. Typically they are tall and slender,
perhaps 18 ins. high, with a slim elegant neck and a
bulging midriff.

Rembrandt. Another painter who has given his name to a
flagon type because of its frequent appearance in his pictures. A typical specimen will stand say 10 ins. high, and
look not unlike some kinds of baluster measures.

Rorcken. Guild jugs in the shape of lidded tumblers.

Schenkkanne. This name appears to have been applied to any flagon which was used for pouring out the decanted wine, whereas the *Schleppkanne* was used for carrying it up from the cellar, and the *Schliefkanne* for passing round the table; it had an outward tapering base, a bronze tap, and ball feet.

Stitzen. This term is used on the Continent to describe a form of flagon with an elegant line which swells out at the base and makes it one of the most firmly-seated vessels ever devised. It is based, like the *Pechkrug* (q.v.), on an earlier staved wooden vessel.

Stubenkanne. A term for a vessel used in a *Stube* or hall— what we should think of as a saloon bar or a club.

Walliserkäntli. Swiss vessels not unlike our baluster measures in shape, with heart-shaped lid. They are usually placed upside-down on shelves with the lids hanging down so that they show off to the best advantage.

BEAKERS

The beaker form is as ancient as any kind of drinking vessel and it would be surprising if we did not find it in pewter. The first mention of it in English records comes at about the end of the sixteenth century: and there are interesting specimens from about the beginning of the seventeenth century ornamented with scrolls of grape-vines and flowers in relief-cast decoration. Some of these bear Royal Stuart emblems and monograms. Later in the century come those engraved with busts of William and Mary, with decorative carnations or tulips.

Abroad, beakers used by the Lutherans as Communion cups often have sketchily engraved pictures of the life of Christ, with dates of around 1710 to 1715. They were also, as already mentioned, used in certain parishes in Britain. In the nineteenth century the English beaker developed horizontal mouldings which served to conceal the join where they were made in two pieces. In Austria and Germany, however, the tourist trade was catered for with a type of beaker which was cast in moulds and turned down

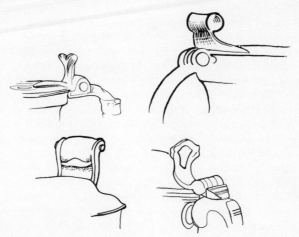

Thumbpieces on measures. 'Bud', 'Hammerhead', 'Chairback', and 'Open'.

inside very thinly. They were sold as souvenirs of such towns as Nuremberg, Dresden, Munich, Cologne, etc. Dutch beakers usually have an additional concave moulding between foot and drum.

MEASURES

'If any man makes or causes to be made any measure pots, commonly called tavern pots, of any less measure than by the standard appointed for the same pots, the defaulter shall also stand on the pillory on three lawful market days according to the order of the city.'

Thus was the pewterer left in no doubt by his own trade Ordinances of the penalties attaching to malpractices in the matter of measures. Today most collections contain at least a few of the measures which the centuries have left behind: and there are some excellent collections of nothing else.

The early records mention different sizes, and give the weights appropriate to each. They refer to such types as Normandy, household and measure pots, stope pots, etc.

The first of those known to us is the baluster shape, found only in pewter and exclusively in the British Isles. As we shall see later, they were admirably designed from the earliest days to circumvent the knavish innkeeper trying to give false measure.

THUMBPIECES

The lidded varieties are generally classified by the shape and nature of the thumbpiece and its attachment, and although there was just as much overlapping in the dates of the various styles, it is possible to see some sort of sequence. The main type in use up to about 1650 is called the 'wedge', after the shape of the attachment running along the top of the lid (below right): sometimes this is accompanied by a ball-shaped thumbpiece, when it is called the 'ball and wedge'; very few genuine examples of these are still in existence. From about 1680 there were thumbpieces shaped as 'buds' and 'hammerheads' (see page 30), and these remained in fashion until the middle of the next century.

(Left) *Jersey measure with twin-acorn thumbpiece.*
(Right) *The English baluster with 'bud'-type thumb-piece.* (Victoria & Albert Museum)

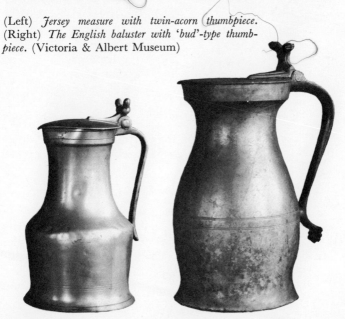

In the early 1700s appeared the 'double volute' which stayed until the nineteenth century.

Scottish pewterers favoured a type which has been called the 'ball and bar', in which the attachment is not wedge-shaped but rectangular. This was in general use by the end of the eighteenth century, and it was followed by the oddly named 'embryo-shell', so called because it was supposed to look like a seashell before it has acquired ridges. A variation of this shape has been named by Mr Ronald Michaelis the 'spade', because it has the shape of the pointed digging implement once universally used here and on the Continent. Scottish measures have a raised flange of metal beneath the lids which prevent them when closed from sliding from side to side, so weakening the hinge.

As already mentioned, the first drinking measures seem also to have been drinking pots, being given names like thurndells, Winchester and Ephraim pints. In the mid fourteenth century there were measures called 'potels' or 'pottels' which seem to have been of two quarts' capacity. A table of the year 1673–4 gives wine measures in weights:

gallon	10 lbs. each
pottle	6 lbs. each
quart	3 lbs. each
pint	2 lbs. each
½ pint	1 lb. each
¼ pint (gill)	8 lbs. per dozen
half ¼ pint, or ½ gill	8 lbs. per dozen

The list does not mention the quarter-gill which is sometimes offered to collectors: Mr Michaelis believes that these are all fakes.

BAFFLING BALUSTERS

The above are the names collectors usually give to baluster measures of the different sizes, but it should be noted that the capacities are not Imperial measures but those of the Old English Wine Measure, which was five-sixths of Im-

32

perial Measure—and incidentally is the present United States Liquid Measure.

When every dent in a measure meant extra profit for the innkeeper or vintner, the Ordinances were careful to lay down standards designed to circumvent tricks of this sort, and the English baluster measure did this admirably. The metal used had to be thick enough to withstand reasonable buffeting, and of course the baluster shape helped here; so did the incised lines found on many measures, which would look out of line if there was a dent. There was no foot-ring, so the base had to be flat; and since the neck was smaller in diameter than the top or foot, one could not insert a plate giving a false bottom. Rings cut into the lid would show if there had been any attempt to hammer the lid down into the measure.

IRISH 'HAYSTACKS'

From Ireland come two highly individual types of measure. There is the 'haystack' or 'harvester'—so called, it seems, after the shapes of the hay- and corn-stacks in that country. There was also the well-known 'noggin', or handleless baluster. The word actually means gill or quarter-pint measure, and as such is common both to Scotland and Ireland; but it is to be found in four sizes—half-pint, quarter-, one-eighth-, and one-sixteenth pint—all Imperial Standard. There are variations in the degree of the curve, and the smallest ones in the set are usually of quite a different shape from the others.

Beer-mug, early eighteenth century. Touch of William Hux of London. 5 ins. high.

33

Mr Cotterell claims that the noggins (or 'naggins') came from around Dublin and the east of Ireland, and that the haystacks were from Cork and the South. The haystack differs from the somewhat similar West Country in the slope of the lip; the latter slopes from front to back and has a fillet round the body; the handle is also different and is attached to the lip instead of the body.

The Bristol or West Country Measure is in fact a quite distinctive type (see page 35) no doubt originating in Bristol's wine and spirit trade. From the mid eighteenth century there have been variations in contour, and the measure was probably not made in pewter after about 1830 —although of course it has been prolifically made in copper and brass since. A set ranges from a gallon to half a gill.

UNIQUE SCOTTISH MEASURES

The earliest of the Scottish measures is the 'pot-bellied' type, found both lidded and unlidded. The style was apparently picked up from the Continent—an interesting instance of direct Scottish contacts with the mainland.

The thumbpiece peculiar to these and other conventional Scottish measures has already been mentioned. Scottish balusters were in general more symmetrical than the English ones. The incised lines are also shallower and usually closer together. In the nineteenth century the most common of these was that with a pear-shaped body and a domed cover, made down to about 1860.

But Scotland offers us two unique measures in the famous 'tappit hen' and the 'thistle'. The first is thought to have picked up its name from the French *topynet*, a measure of capacity, although the measures appear in different sizes. Here we have one of those anomalies like the Chinese porcelain known as Oriental Lowestoft, which had nothing whatever to do with the east coast port.

Tappit hens are found in a range of sizes with both Imperial and Scottish Standards, but they were originally made in three sizes only; the true tappit hen of 1 Scots

34

pint capacity (equal to 3 English Imperial pints), the 'chopin' ($1\frac{1}{2}$ Imperial pints)—from the French *chopine*—and the 'mutchkin' ($\frac{3}{4}$ Imperial pint). As English measures were adopted in the nineteenth century so these were made in the same forms. The earliest dated tappit hen seems to be a chopin of 1669 in the National Museum of Antiquities of Scotland, Edinburgh. The crested tappit hens—with a crest or knob in the centre of the lid—were made in the Scottish measures only, say, from 1780. There are also lidless ones, with unslotted hinged lugs. Tappit hens are such popular shapes that there have been many reproductions of them—and not only in pewter.

The thistle measure appears in the first quarter of the nineteenth century, and can be found in sizes from the Imperial pint down to the Scots half-gill. A great many of them were destroyed, for by a thoughtful act of 1907 all measures had to empty themselves when tilted to 120 degrees —which the thistle failed to do.

CAPACITY SEALS
Early baluster measures bore a capacity mark or seal impressed on the cover of the body. It was a crown with the monogram 'hR'—the small and large letters are important.

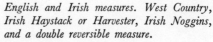

English and Irish measures. West Country, Irish Haystack or Harvester, Irish Noggins, and a double reversible measure.

35

One school of thought maintains that it indicates conformity to a standard laid down in the reign of Henry VIII; but there seems to be no evidence in support of this. Moreover, a very similar mark appears on measures made much later than this reign, for example, at the end of the seventeenth century. A variation of the mark, with both initials in capitals, appears together with the City of London arms upon measures of as late as the end of the eighteenth century. There are also measures bearing the monograms 'W.R.' and 'A.R.' presumably indicating the reigns of William III and Anne respectively. Mr Michaelis has suggested that the 'hR' mark might refer to 'household Royal, Rex, or Regina' since there was once a complaint about false measure, even though the piece was sealed by the Clerk of the Market of the Queen's Household.

Baluster measures are not often found with capacity seals, although legal stamping of Winchester measures was enforced by an Act of 1790. But it was not until the introduction of the Imperial system of weights and measures in 1824 that steps could seriously be taken to enforce correct measures. From then on, counties and boroughs sent their inspectors round testing measures and drinking vessels, and stamping them with a local symbol together with letters or numbers signifying the year. In 1877 the mark was standardized for the whole country as a Royal Crown with the sovereign's initials and a number for the local authority and a letter for the date. One sometimes comes across measures and tankards with a whole row of these marks, extending over many years.

Scottish measures. Thistle, Pot-bellied, Pear-shaped, and Crested tappit hen.

3. At High Table

PLATES, DISHES, AND CHARGERS

Medieval folk were good trenchermen, and trenchermen needed trenchers. What exactly was a trencher, a platter, or 'chargeour'—to say nothing of a 'King's Dish', a 'voyder' or a 'dobeler'?

The early records abound in such terms, and give the most explicit details of the weights they should conform to, and the methods of making. But—as already seen with tankards—one of the nicest puzzles facing modern collectors and scholars is to discover exactly which of the surviving pieces these records describe, if indeed they have survived.

The new specialist collector will no doubt take a deep dive into these waters and perhaps add something to the pool of knowledge. For the rest of us, we may simply note that before pewter, people used wooden platters and dishes or chargers—which were not always round, but sometimes square, with a round depression and a small well for salt; also wooden bowls of various kinds. When they came to be made in pewter, these items were classed together as flatware or sadware; and by Ordinance they had to be made of fine pewter. Today's collectors seem to by-pass the medieval terms mentioned above and class their sadware into plates when they are up to 10 ins. in diameter; dishes when they are up to 18 ins., and chargers when they are larger than this.

There are some plates with shallow bowls dug up at Guy's Hospital, London, which bear a punched crowned feather on the rim: these seem to be of Tudor date. Plates with broad rims have usually been called patens, but as has been pointed out elsewhere (see page 24), this ecclesiastical use can by no means be taken for granted: such items would have been just as suitable for domestic use. A

37

distinctive type whose name dates back to the mid fifteenth century is the 'Cardinal's Hat', which has a broad brim and a deep well.

Reeded moulding round the edges of the rims of plates is of some help in dating. Throughout most of the first half of the seventeenth century the rims were plain, or had a simple incised fillet, while from then until the end of the century multiple reeding was cut by gouging out grooves while the plate was turned on a lathe (in which the reeding stands above the rim). In the first half of the eighteenth century, this multiple reeding was replaced by a simpler moulded reeding, while from then on to the end of pewter plate-making the rim was left quite plain but was thickened on the underside. Plates which bear the maker's mark struck three times are probably of continental origin.

As one might expect, Baroque fashions of the eighteenth century brought variations in plate shapes. There were six-, eight-, or ten-sided plates, at first plain but later with multiple

Pewter dish cast in relief with scenes from the story of the Prodigal Son, inset with a medallion in Limoges enamel. French, about 1550, $17\frac{11}{16}$ ins. diameter. (Victoria & Albert Museum)

Porringer. Late seventeenth century. Cover with lion feet. (Victoria & Albert Museum)

reeding or beading. There were gadrooned or wavy-edged plates in the manner of contemporary silver and porcelain, with five, six, or eight lobes.

Marriage plates, with the initials of the two Christian names and the surname, as in delftware, are known and there is also a pewter version of the 'Merryman' series, whereby each plate has a separate inscription, as follows:

1. What is a merry man?
2. Let him do what he can.
3. To entertain his guests.
4. With wine and merry jests.
5. But if his wife do frown.
6. All merriment goes down.

But watch for fakes: these words have sometimes been added to otherwise genuine old plates.

PORRINGERS

The porringer is a favourite with collectors—when it can be found. It is a small bowl with either one or two flat handles sticking out from the rim in a way which justifies its description, in the records for 1556, as an 'eare disshe'.

The earliest of those known is the 'Elizabethan' type, with handles rather like a cloverleaf—possibly this is the 'three-leafe-grasse eare'. There are later versions—to be seen in the Guildhall Museum, London—with the 'flower delice' or fleur-de-lis decoration mentioned in the same entry.

From this beginning flowed all the decorated handles which have so delighted connoisseurs by their charm and variety, and lifted this humble utensil into the realm of commemorative pewter. But so far as this country's pewter was concerned, this two-handled porringer was a false dawn: with the close of the Elizabethan era, British porringers nearly always contented themselves with one handle: those with two were generally of continental manufacture.

In early Stuart days the porringer tended to have a flat-based bowl, sometimes with a boss in the centre, and with straight sides sloping outwards. However, from about Commonwealth times for perhaps a century, this was superseded by the bowl with curved sides and a small collar to the brim.

Much coveted are the splendid porringers made for commemorative purposes. They seem to have appeared quite suddenly in this country in the time of William and Mary. It is very reasonable to suppose, as Mr Michaelis has pointed out, that this sudden eruption into elaborate decoration—and resumption of two handles on British porringers—may have arisen as the result of the coming of the Prince of Orange to these shores.

One presumes that, like the continental examples—which closely followed the lidded *equelles* in ordinary use—all these porringers originally had covers, often with knobs ornamented on the lids, which, when the cover was reversed, served as a stand. Sometimes these knobs take the form of a cockerel or a lion, sometimes cherubs holding a crown. Designs were cast into both the bowl and the cover, usually with related themes. For example, William III and Mary II appear conjointly, as well as the Duke of Marlborough and Queen Anne. There seems to be good reason to believe that in some way these handsome vessels, though made in Britain, owed their designs to Dutch pewterers, perhaps by emigration.

Salts. Mid eighteenth century, 3⅛ ins. high; late seventeenth century, 2⅜ ins. high, maker's touch 'L.S.'; dated 1746. (Victoria & Albert Museum)

Unique to Scotland—in name at any rate—is a version of a porringer called the 'quaich', though it is also to be found in France. It has quite plain ears and varies in size from about 3½ ins. up to 9 or 10 ins. No doubt the smaller ones were for drinking, and the larger ones for porridge.

It should be mentioned, however, that both quaiches and the more richly adorned kind of porringers have been reproduced in quantity—and long enough ago already to have acquired a patina.

One has used the word 'porringer' exclusively so far, but in fact the plainer bowls which usually go under this name, when they are small in size, are sometimes thought of as wine-tasters. Porringers have also been called 'bleeding bowls', or 'blood porringers'. There are other types of vessel which are also called bleeding bowls, notably one which looks rather like a saucepan with a curled-up handle, which is sometimes measured off in ounces: there is also the barber's bowl with an arc cut in the rim for the neck —barbers bled their customers as well as shaved them.

There is not a great deal of difference between the covered porringer and the caudle cup: in fact silver collectors tend to use the term 'porringer' for this form, which is also found in pottery and porcelain. Caudle, a drink mainly given to invalids or women in childbirth, was made up of oatmeal mixed with hot wine or beer, then sweetened or spiced.

Sometimes the underside of the ears of porringers are more carefully decorated than the upper—suggesting that

41

Pepper-pot engraved with the badge of the 43rd Regiment of Foot. Early eighteenth century, 6¼ ins. high. Sugar-caster. Early eighteenth century, 8 ins. high. (Victoria & Albert Museum)

they were meant to be seen in this way when hung on a sideboard or shelf. One would have thought that the way the ears join the bowl puts an undue strain on it, but they are usually very toughly made, and there is one type which has a strengthening wedge section under the handle.

SALTS

Next to plates the most conspicuous item on the table was the saler or salt—what we now tautologically call the salt-cellar. Silver and gold salts—once defining a guest's social ranking above or below it—are well known, but the pewter ones seem to have been modest affairs. Square trenchers, as we have seen, sometimes had a depression for salt: from this it was presumably but a step to the trencher salt, round, square or triangular, with a central depression: sometimes they had more than one depression, perhaps for spices.

From the second half of the seventeenth century come several apparently new forms. There was the spool-shape, sometimes with a lid, but often having three raised fingers over which a small linen cloth could be draped. About the same time appear the various versions of the capstan salt, round or octagonal, plain, beaded or gadrooned. These very practical affairs, with their heavy bases to prevent the unlucky accident, were very popular all through the rest of the century. From about 1700 onwards there were new types, one a deeply welled bowl, another remarkably like a modern ashtray, a newer version of the trencher, and the cup mounted on a stand.

Just as the bases of the older salts were often used for candlesticks as well (see page 53) so the feet of these cup salts may well have been inverted and used for the lids of some domed tankards.

Peppers and mustards come in a variety of shapes, the former sometimes very similar to the pounce-pots mentioned on page 56. They also appear in the form of owls or pug-dogs. Complete lidded condiment-boxes are known. Sugar-bowls in the scalloped shapes of Louis XV as well as in the more formal styles of Louis XVI are to be found on the Continent.

SPOONS

Spoons find their specialist collectors, and they are full of interest. In many ways they follow those in silver and may be dated roughly from these—which, of course, bear the usual silver hall-marks. But the earliest ones take us back much further, into the fourteenth or even the thirteenth century. They are, in fact, some of the oldest specimens of pewter—excluding the product of classical times—which have come down to us.

Down to the middle of the seventeenth century English spoons invariably had fig-shaped bowls. The stems were round or six-sided, and nearly always terminated in a decorative knop. It is by these knops or the absence of them that collectors generally classify their spoons.

Among the most common specimens to survive is the 'slip-top' or 'slipped in the stalk' spoon, where the stem is cut off, usually diagonally, like a scion used in grafting. Perhaps the very earliest, however, are the 'ball knop', 'diamond point' and the 'acorn', all of which appear to have been about in the thirteenth and fourteenth centuries.

The next century produced several interesting knops. Not to be found in silver, apparently, is the 'horned head-dress',

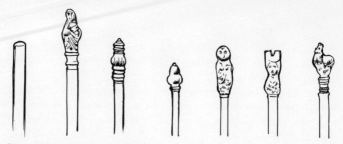

Spoon knops. Slip-top or Slipped in the Stalk, Apostle, Baluster, Acorn, Monk's Head, Horned Head-dress, Chanticleer, Maidenhead, Horse's hoof, Seal-top, Lion sejant, and Melon.

which shows the head and bust of a girl wearing the horned or crescent-shaped head-dress of the time of Joan of Arc: it can be seen in many paintings of the period. Another well-known type of those days is the 'maidenhead', which again shows a woman's head and is thought to represent the Virgin Mary. Other knops include the 'wrythen', in which the ball or cone top is twisted, the 'melon', the 'hexagonal', the 'lion sejant' (or sitting lion), the 'baluster' and the 'stump end'. A rare one shows a monk with a cowl over his head and his hands folded before him.

'Apostle' spoons, like those in silver, were made all the way through from, say, 1450 to 1700, although the full set of thirteen (with the Master) has never, I believe, been found in pewter. They were given at christenings, with the appropriate name-saint for the child. 'Seal-tops' describe themselves, and there were also pewter versions of the 'woodnose' or wild man.

The 'horse's hoof' seems to have been one of the later additions before the Civil War, but during the Commonwealth there came in that very austere spoon the 'Puritan', which had an oval bowl and a flat straight stem with no ornament of any kind. After the Restoration the stem was made broader, giving the 'rounded-end', and then the 'notched and shaped', leading to the 'split-end', otherwise

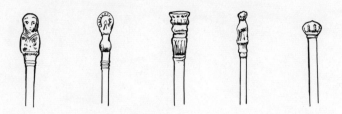

called the 'trifid' or '*pied-de-biche*'. Then followed some more elaborate spoons with cast decoration on the stems and the backs of the bowls. Sometimes they showed effigies of the monarchs, such as Charles II, William and Mary, or Queen Anne. The later Hanoverian spoons portraying George II or Queen Charlotte have longer stems and narrower bowls. Later this developed into the egg-shape, with perhaps a ridge running up the stem.

Ladles are to be found in pewter, those from the Continent being larger than the English, also shorter and thicker in the handle.

TWO-HANDLED CUPS

More appropriately treated here than among the flagons and tankards are the two-handled cups which are variously called porringers, wassail bowls, caudle cups, posset pots, toasting cups, grace cups or wine cups.

Caudle was a kind of custard made of oatmeal or biscuit mixed with hot wine or beer, and as already mentioned was the equivalent of gruel given to invalids or women in child-bed. The Swiss version of the caudle cup was the Kindbett-schüsseli (see page 28), which might take the form of a shallow dish with feet on it and also on the cover.

There seems no doubt that our ancestors were much less eager to classify these items by use than are modern collectors. After all, leaving aside silver, a well-made pot in fine pewter was not a cheap item for the kind of household which used this metal, and it is a reasonable conclusion that the same vessel would have been used for different purposes.

Smaller sizes would obviously be more suitable for porridge or caudle, and larger ones for toasting at the table. Much of the confusion may have arisen because caudle cups which have lost their covers and stands are assumed never to have had them, and so become classified as wassail bowls or loving cups.

So far as shapes are concerned, the early ones date from about the 1660s, and have straight sides tapering towards the mouth—worthy consorts of the lovely Stuart tankards. They show the typical contemporary designs of birds and flowers in wriggled work or with engraved cyphers, and these are among the pieces which bore imitation silver hall-marks.

When they were used as wassail bowls or loving cups the custom was, as at banquets today, to pass the cup from guest to guest, the grasping of one handle each symbolizing friendship: there are some with three handles, a form which persisted right down to the Victorian tankard.

By the time of Queen Anne, the two-handled cup appears in the early tulip-shape (see above) of the contemporary tankards, but rather wider in the bowl, as one might expect. The gadrooned work and the decorative scrolled handles of the specimen already referred to seem to have been followed later in the century by a simpler form, as shown in the other cup above, with a flattened thumbrest on the much thicker handles of the period. One notes here, too, the beginnings of the footed cup which developed into the loving cup proper: this term seems not to have been used before about 1800. Smaller ones, like those in pottery, bearing the initials of couples, may have been used as wedding-gifts.

Two-handled mugs. (Left) about 1684, (right) about 1730. (Victoria & Albert Museum)

(Above) Beer-jug, engraved 'WLW' and bearing imitation silver hall-marks. Maker's initials,'R.M.' Late eighteenth century. (Above right) Beer-jug of about 1800. (Below left) Coffee-pot with wooden knop and handle, German, eighteenth century. (Below right) Jug engraved 'I.G.', and once the property of Paddy Green of Evans Supper Rooms, Covent Garden. Late eighteenth century. (Victoria & Albert Museum)

4. Sacred and Ceremonial

Pewter was used a great deal in churches, and in some parishes survives even to this day. One first hears of pewter chalices and patens—used in the service of the Mass for wine and wafers—in Church ordinances made towards the end of the eleventh century, when wooden vessels were banned and pewter allowed if the parish could afford nothing better.

CHALICES AND PATENS

Pewter chalices and patens now found are likely to be of post-Reformation date. The word 'chalice' is used indiscriminately by collectors to describe both the classical chalice-shape with a wide bowl—as found in the tombs—and the later goblet-shaped Communion cup. But there are also post-Reformation examples which follow the old shape, especially in Scottish parishes. Sometimes they have a cover, and this may also serve for a footed paten (see page 50).

Pair of altar candlesticks with iron prickets, and a chrismatory. (Victoria & Albert Museum)

Every kind of goblet-shape is to be found, including even the cylindrical 'rummer'. There are also chalices in the form of beakers. In the absence of an inscription it is impossible to distinguish between these Communion cups and those used as ordinary goblets for the household. The same is true of patens.

The earliest of the known shapes are small and circular, with a flat rim and a deep well. The post-Reformation patens tend to have a shallower well, and are often used as stands for flagons—a necessity in view of the fact that so many flagons had no lip for easy pouring.

There are footed patens of a larger type than those used as covers. Some of them are marked or inscribed, but the great majority are not. These 'tazzas', as they are sometimes called, look rather like cake-stands.

Flagons have already been mentioned in another place (see pages 22–9): as with chalices and patens, there seems to be no real assurance without an inscription that a particular piece was made for ecclesiastical use. In fact, churches in the poorer parishes seem often to have been content to use tankards or even measures—sometimes to the irritation of visiting bishops.

OTHER ALTAR VESSELS

Pewter was used also for the cruets or small covered vessels for wine and water at the altar, but very few of those which survive are certainly of English origin. They are sometimes marked on the lids with an 'A' for *aqua*, and a 'V' for *vinum*: forgeries of these are reported. This also applies to wafer-boxes and chrismatories, vessels used to contain consecrated oil. These are sometimes single, but are also found joined in pairs or triples, or in a box like caddies in a tea-chest.

Continental countries are far richer in such items—though here too the collector must keep his wits about him. The pyx, or box for storing the consecrated bread, appears in various shapes, including the cylindrical and hexagonal,

Chalice with footed cover as paten;
and paten with Communion cup.

usually surmounted by a cross or some other emblem or figure. They can sometimes be confused with the more elaborate sort of lidded salt. The ciborium is a form of chalice, with a crucifix on the lid: it is used for passing round the consecrated bread.

There are incense-boats in pewter, and small reliquaries for holding holy relics; also holy-water stoups sometimes made to hang on walls: they often bear representations of the Crucifixion, or of the Virgin and Child. Small vessels carried by pilgrims for holding consecrated oil or earth have been found in considerable numbers, as have pilgrims' badges.

ALMSDISHES

Almsdishes were made in pewter, but however hopeful the owner may be of proving one-time use in church, many are indistinguishable from domestic wares. Some rare types have an enamel boss in the centre.

Among the small pewter associated with the Church are tokens issued by the Scottish Churches to those wishing to take Holy Communion. The earliest of them, used in the Presbyterian Church, seem to date from the end of the sixteenth century. Sometimes they were simply small rectangles of lead an inch or so square punched with an iron stamp; or they may be cast in moulds with a design cut in one side. Later the Churches used tokens struck from dies in the same way as medallions.

Baptismal bowls sometimes bear witness to use in this ceremony by still standing in their wrought-iron brackets.

But there seem to be far more about than ever could have come out of churches alone; in any case, such a shape was well adapted to domestic use.

PROCESSIONAL STAVES

If you had been present at the funeral of the Duke of Wellington in 1852 you would have seen in that splendidly mournful procession to St Paul's a line of inky-suited mutes carrying black rods. Each one bore at its end a phoenix rising from the ashes moulded in pewter; there were also other mountings of the same metal. These maces, or processional staves, were often used on ceremonial occasions, and they took many forms. Some had tops like the bowl of a goblet, surrounded by a cross or some other symbol: or there might be a ball, or diamond-shaped head. A hand, or the curve of a shepherd's crook, suggests trade uses, and of course the Beadle of the Pewterers' Company would have had a pewter head to his stave. A stave with a three-faced figure is said to have been the wand of a tipstaff.

CANDLESTICKS AND LAMPS

Some of the finest shapes in pewter—and nothing could be better devised to set off a garnish of plates on a sideboard—are to be found in the great variety of candle-sticks.

Records suggest that candlesticks were in use in abbeys, parish churches and noblemen's houses from at least the thirteenth century, and their story runs down to today. In the Archives of the Pewterers' Company for 1612–13 weights are given for named types

The Grainger Candlestick. Cast relief decoration of the Royal Arms, the Pewterers' Company of London, and the name William Graing(e)r. Dated 1616, 9¼ ins. high. (Victoria & Albert Museum)

51

Candlesticks. Mid eighteenth century, 8¼ ins. high; last quarter seventeenth century, 7¾ ins. high, maker's touch 'SB' over a star; late seventeenth century, 6½ ins. high; first quarter eighteenth century, 6⅞ ins. high; late seventeenth century, 5⅞ ins. high; early nineteenth century, 8¾ ins. high; and about 1830 (Victoria & Albert Museum)

of candlesticks like 'ordinarie highe', 'great middle', 'small wryteing'; there are also candlesticks with 'bawles'. The 'great bell' or 'high bell' candlesticks seem to refer to those as seen in the first specimen from the Victoria and Albert Museum. The 'bell', of course, refers to the shape of the foot.

The earliest of all the types existing today is the simple pricket, with a point on which the tallow candle was stuck, but tyro collectors should be warned that many of these 'Elizabethan' candlesticks offered today were made in the days of the Queen who reigned three centuries later.

The first of the conventional candlesticks seems to have been the trumpet base, but very nearly contemporary with this was a shape with a circular base having depressions to catch the molten tallow and a plain or slightly knopped stem finishing in a plain socket with an everted, or outward-turning rim. The earliest dated one we have of this type is the beautiful Grainger Candlestick in the Victoria and Albert Museum, which is shown on page 51. Here, unusually, British pewter appears in an elaborately ornamental form. The cast decoration showing the arms of the Pewterers'

Company and the date 1616 commemorates William
Grainger, who was made a Freeman Pewterer of the London
Company in 1597, and successfully served in the office of
Searcher (or Examiner), Steward, Renter Warden, and
finally in 1638, Upper Warden. There are also some rare
dodecagonal, or twelve-sided candlesticks deeply scalloped
on base and drip-tray.

As was the case with tankards, the second half of the
seventeenth century brought a variety of styles. There were
square bases, with similarly shaped or round pillars.
Octagonal bases were popular up to the end of the William
and Mary era, when the central drip-tray tended to give
place to a baluster effect. At the turn of the century there
were tall balusters like those in brass, having a rod in the
pillar for pushing out small remnants of tallow. This style
was extremely long-lived, continuing well into Victorian
days.

All these 'Jacobeans', as they seem to be generically
called, are hard to find. Many of those seen here are of
Dutch and other continental origin, and there are some
which seem to have come from the Scandinavian countries.
But specimens from the latter half of the eighteenth century
and the first of the nineteenth are fairly plentiful.

ECONOMIZING ON MOULDS
Sometimes the bases of candlesticks are of exactly of the same
form as those of salts: clearly the same mould was used for

53

both. There is also at least one instance where a very tall altar candlestick has been made by joining two castings from the same pillar mould, inverting one on the other and adding an extra wide drip-tray on the top. Stems of candlesticks have also been used for a ciborium.

All this is a very natural process in a craft where moulds were among the costliest items of manufacture, so much so that they were handed down from father to son for generations. This, of course, is another reason why styles in some places should have continued to exist long after they had disappeared elsewhere. A pewterer had to think twice before abandoning moulds which had cost him or his forebears real money, and it was only the more prosperous and successful pewterers who could afford to be innovators.

Looking abroad, collectors of candlesticks will be interested in the famous Heemskirk specimens. In the year 1556 the Dutch navigators Jacob van Heemskirk and William Barendtsz made their gallant but unsuccessful attempt on the North-East Passage, the Arctic route to China. They spent the winter at Nova Zembla, where Barendtsz died, and the rest of the expedition made their way back to Amsterdam only after suffering the greatest privations. Behind them at Nova Zembla they left a good deal of equipment, and in 1876, over three hundred years later, this was found by a sea captain from Hammerfest and an Englishman, Dr Gardner. Among it were no fewer than twenty candlesticks of the type known in Holland as *Kraagkandelaar*, or 'collar candlesticks', usually found in brass and occasionally in bronze. The finders returned them to the explorers' native land, and they may now be seen in the Rijksmuseum at Amsterdam.

Similar candlesticks have been found in England within the last forty years. In 1930 during excavations on the site of an old plumbers' shop in the Newborough district of Scarborough, labourers found a battered but intact specimen of one with a base like a salt of the era. Others were collected from various sources between 1830 and 1870 by the grandfather of Mr Richard Neate, who described them in an article in the *Connoisseur* in 1934.

Altar candlesticks are not always separately identifiable, but there are holy lamps on chains bearing a permanent light. There is also the Jewish 'synagogue' or Sabbath lamp hanging from a rim. It is shaped as a seven-pointed star with seven wicks for the days of the week and was lit at sunset on Fridays, and on the eve of a festival. The Maccabean, or 'Chanoeka' lamp celebrating the victories of Judas Maccabeus, has eight oil-lamps in a container, with a ninth above from which the others are lit, one on each consecutive night.

Other lighting equipment to be found in pewter includes 'clocks' which originally had a glass oil-reservoir with graduations marked to show the hours.

5. Oddments and Oddities

Orthodox pewter collectors tend to think of the early Victorian era as the 'decline'—such and such a shape, they say, was made down to the 'end', meaning somewhere about 1830.

But pewter, in fact, continued to be made, even if in reduced quantities, and for the general collectors referred to in the Introduction, there are scores of byways to explore.

INKSTANDS

We have seen (page 52) that there were such things as 'small wryteing' candles. Not far away from it on the desk would be the inkstand, or standish, as it used to be called. The earliest ones seem to be those round types without lids, with moulding on the foot, and holes round the rim for the pens. The 'loggerhead' type has a broad flange round the foot to steady it, in case the heavy cuff of your eighteenth-century sleeve brushed against the pens.

More elaborate inkstands came later, and in their full development closely followed silver models. One type was a rectangular box with a tray below for the quill-pens and the 'penknife' with which to trim them. Above the tray were separately lidded compartments holding the ink, the wafers for sealing the folded letter, and pounce or sand.

Most ubiquitous of all, however, were the open trays,

Inkstand with drawers and removable top.

56

which were, in effect, platforms with depressions for the various containers, which might also be of pewter or of glass. Sometimes the tray stood upon lion's head feet.

SNUFF-BOXES AND RASPS

Pewter has long been favoured by snuff-takers, and wonderful are the forms which the pewterers have sometimes devised for them. There are boxes shaped as pistols, as cockle-shells and ladies' slippers; but there is also a very wide range of more orthodox boxes. Mostly they are rectangular, more rarely round or oval. Usually in the best-quality pewter—because of the inevitable wear on hinges—some are cast in two sections with the lid added, others are from a single piece with the sides bent up and soldered. They may also have separate sides embossed with some design, or stamped in light relief. There may be panels in some other metal, like pinchbeck or brass. The insides of earlier types were gilded, but later they were painted gold.

French, Dutch and German specimens are to be found, but in the absence of marks on most of them, attribution is a matter of guesswork. Religious subjects and genre scenes usually point to a continental origin.

That portable snuff-making factory, the 'sneeshing miln' or Scottish mull, has been described in another book in this series (ALL KINDS OF SMALL BOXES): it must also be offered to pewter collectors. Briefly it consisted of the horn of a ram,

Tobacco-box, Dutch, dated 1751, $5\frac{7}{8}$ ins. high. (Victoria & Albert Museum)

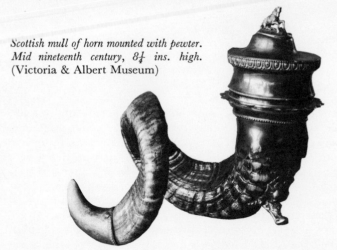

*Scottish mull of horn mounted with pewter.
Mid nineteenth century, 8¼ ins. high.*
(Victoria & Albert Museum)

or cow, or the hoof of a deer, with sharp ridges cut inside so as to provide a means of grating a plug of tobacco and so producing snuff at minimum expense. It has metal caps and other mountings which are often of pewter, and is accompanied by a set of apparatus—a snuff-spoon, a small mallet, a rake and a hare's foot for dusting the snuff off a beard or moustache.

TOBACCO REQUISITES

The collector of tobacco requisites also finds fulfilment in pewter. There are tobacco-boxes of many shapes, and there are also small match-boxes of the sort made throughout Victorian times. There were those made to contain the uncertain phosphorus matches of mid Victorian times, and also the little vesta-boxes which gentlemen liked to have dangling on their watch-chains. These were in a great variety of shapes and guises, from birds to shoes, and from soda-siphons to fiddles. Cigar-cases are also to be found in pewter.

The collector of miniatures or 'toys', those sometimes very charming replicas of everyday objects, also finds his quarry in pewter. There is tiny flatware, using hammered plate, from the eighteenth century; but in Victorian days whole tea, coffee, and dinner sets were made, and they were enormously popular for the huge doll's houses of the era. Small pewter tankards are to be found on the walls of the kitchen of the doll's house in the Victoria and Albert Museum, as well as miniature candlesticks and other items.

KITCHEN WARES

In times when brass and copper kettles and other kitchen wares are avidly collected we must not forget the very redoubtable part played in this field by pewter. There were 'warmers and coolers' designed for the confectioner's shop to keep soups and pastry warm in winter and ice-creams and iced water cool in summer; there were oval meat dishes, hot-water dishes and plates, butter- and gravy-boats with wicker handles, and 'melon-shaped moulds for icing puddings'.

The one foreign firm to show a wide range of pewter articles at the Great Exhibition of 1851, incidentally, was Franz Hirsche, of Brunn, Moravia, who brought over

(Left) *Tobacco-jar with touch of Robert Pitt of London, late eighteenth century, 6⅛ ins. high.* (Right) *Shaving-dish with maker's touch 'IH' in a shield, late seventeenth century, 10⅝ ins. diameter.* (Victoria & Albert Museum)

(Left) *Pocket flask, engraved with the name of the owner, Edward Barrett, Lynn 1799, 4¾ ins. high.* (Right) *Tea-caddy, with a touch probably belonging to one of the Duncomb family of Birmingham, second quarter of the eighteenth century, 5¾ ins. high.* (Victoria & Albert Museum)

church lamps, tea services, writing materials, chafing-dishes and cooking vessels, the latter being described as a 'novelty'.

BRITANNIA METAL

Here we must say something about Britannia metal. It is a term which tends to horrify orthodox collectors of pewter, partly because they regard it as a totally inferior alloy, with none of the qualities of true pewter, and partly because it was one of the chief agents in the decline of their beloved metal. It offered a cheaper substitute for both silver and Sheffield plate—and so seduced those whose household wares had hitherto been of pewter.

All the same, it has its adherents. Its chief ingredient, after tin, is antimony, a hard brittle metal which takes a high polish like silver and, what is equally important, makes it possible to spin or cast the alloy into the same kind of shapes which were made in silver and Sheffield plate.

This meant that the alloy often shows the fine patterns of the early years of the nineteenth century. Many pieces also carry the 'bright-cut' engraving used in silver, and this has long been appreciated on the Continent.

Britannia metal found in the shops today—and usually offered in all innocence as pewter—consists mostly of tea- and coffee-pots, jugs, sucriers, etc. They are usually marked

60

on the bottom with the name of some such manufacturer as Dixon & Sons, Kirkby, Smith & Co., Joseph Wolstenholme, and others.

There is also often a pattern number and the word 'Sheffield', where much of it was made.

Later in the century, Britannia metal was used as a base for electro-plating, when it bears the initials E.P.B.M.—Electro-plated Britannia Metal.

Unless this fate has also overtaken Britannia wares in the United States, that country should be a happy hunting-ground for specimens of mid-Victorian Britannia: not only were British firms like Dixons busily exporting wares thence at that time, but thriving native 'whitesmiths' like the Bartons of Taunton (Massachusetts) produced pieces in enormous volume, sometimes of an astonishing lushness and exoticism—witness the teapots shown on page 64.

Dutch urn, with painted scenes after Watteau. Mid eighteenth century, 14½ ins. high. (Victoria & Albert Museum)

6. Art Pewter

After lingering tenuously on for several decades within these limited fields—though a quota of Communion or commemorative plate, of tankards with glass bottoms for sporting trophies or gifts was still being produced—pewter suddenly, about the year 1890, found a new lease of life in an entirely unexpected direction.

This was the era of the Arts and Crafts movement, led by William Morris and his disciples, who were finding new interest in traditional methods of craftsmanship and ordinary everyday materials. It lead the way to the use of pewter in 'art manufactures' in the styles currently being evolved in England, Belgium and the United States which culminated in Art Nouveau.

Now enjoying a vogue among collectors, Art Nouveau embodies long asymmetrical curves covering whole surfaces, or twisting forms into strange folds, often built up on animal or plant forms, but always moving and writhing and endlessly sprouting. For a long time critics referred to its 'sagging curves' and 'boneless wonders': but today admiring books are written about it and exhibitions are held to display its products. One such held in the summer of 1964 at the Brighton Museum, the first ever held, but closely followed by one at the Piccadilly Gallery, London, showed several pieces of pewter made by Liberty & Co. of London about the year 1900. How close this firm was to the Art Nouveau movement in their 'art manufactures' is seen in the fact that in Italy it went under the name *Stile Liberty*. From their Birmingham works there came to the Regent Street shop a host of furnishing and decorating articles designed with the new feeling, among them pewter trays, biscuit-boxes, bowls, jugs, tankards quite unlike any seen in the old days, even picture-frames, ewers and wash-basins.

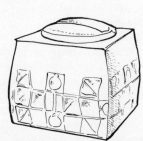

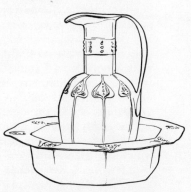

Early - twentieth - century art pewter. German candlestick with hollow column adapted for electric light; English hot-water jug with ornament in low relief; English biscuit-box; and Scottish ewer and wash-basin, designed by George Logan and shown at the Glasgow International Exhibition, 1901.

Among examples of their 'Tudric' wares, as they called them, shown at Brighton there were the biscuit-box shown above, vases decorated with panels of coloured enamels and flowers in relief, a salver with five embossed motifs inset with mother-of-pearl on the rim, and an ink-well with 'Celtic' decoration in relief. There were also pewter crumb-scoops, cake-dishes, a rose-bowl with con-ventionalized leaves and tendrils, some of the leaves being in blue-green enamel. This was also used on spill-vases and a fine circular salver with a border of formalized flowers, leaves and tendrils. A pewter clock had a coloured enamel face. The ewer and basin illustrated above, made by Mr George Logan, was shown at the Glasgow Exhibition, which also featured Chinese lantern bells with swirling

63

tentacles of ornament, and bedroom furniture inlaid with ebony and pewter—always a happy combination.

In Britain, Art Nouveau was generally ridden with a very tight rein, but on the Continent it ran freely and extravagantly. In Germany the firm of J. P. Kayser produced wares of eccentric forms, stamping them with the name 'Kayserzinn'—perhaps intended as an echo of the early 'Edelzinn'. Walter Scherf and Lichtingers were other concerns engaged in making such wares as these.

Odd as the German forms were, their decoration was fairly restrained, often relying on simple geometrical leaf patterns. In France, on the other hand, no holds were barred, and pewter vied with Gallé glass and other 'art manufactures' in exploiting the new ideas to the full. Thus trays would have handles of openwork twigs curling back on to the main piece as leaves. There were teapot-stands like fountains, inkwells like burial-urns, vases with naked drunken bacchae, three-dimensional frogs crouching beside iris heads. A famous plaque called 'L'Onde' (The Wave) shows a drowning Pre-Raphaelite woman with long hair which swirled as furiously as everything else.

A few years ago *bibelots* of this sort could be found in places like the Marché aux Puces in Paris, for no very great sums. But now that Art Nouveau is 'in' again, these pieces have been shown at exhibitions, and priced themselves up into the Bond Street range. Perhaps the pewter collector interested in moving into this department would be advised to wait until this current enthusiasm has been replaced by a more critical mood—and a craze for something else.

American Britannia metal teapots.
Mid nineteenth century.